EARTH**ROCKS!**
GEYSERS

BY SARA GILBERT

CREATIVE EDUCATION • CREATIVE PAPERBACKS

Published by Creative Education and Creative Paperbacks
P.O. Box 227, Mankato, Minnesota 56002
Creative Education and Creative Paperbacks are
imprints of The Creative Company
www.thecreativecompany.us

Design and production by Chelsey Luther
Art direction by Rita Marshall
Printed in the United States of America

Photographs by Alamy (Inge Johnsson), Dreamstime (TMarchev,
Minyun Zhou), Getty Images (Daniel Viñé Garcia, Izzet Keribar, Michael
Melford, Bryan Mullennix, Westend61, Franz Wogerer), iStockphoto
(arianarama, bennymarty, Riishede, Sergey_Krasnoshchokov), Spoon
Graphics (Chris Spooner)

Library of Congress Cataloging-in-Publication Data
Names: Gilbert, Sara.
Title: Geysers / Sara Gilbert.
Series: Earth Rocks!
Includes bibliographical references and index.
Summary: An elementary exploration of geysers, focusing on the
geological evidence that helps explain how and where they form and
spotlighting famous examples, such as Yellowstone's Old Faithful.
Identifiers: ISBN 978-1-60818-893-2 (hardcover) / ISBN 978-1-62832-
509-6 (pbk) / ISBN 978-1-56660-945-6 (eBook)

This title has been submitted for CIP processing under
LCCN 2017937619.

CCSS: RI.1.1, 2, 4, 5, 6, 7; RI.2.2, 5, 6, 7, 10; RI.3.1, 5, 7, 8; RF.1.1, 3, 4; RF.2.3, 4

First Edition HC 9 8 7 6 5 4 3 2 1
First Edition PBK 9 8 7 6 5 4 3 2 1

Pictured on cover: *Fly Geyser, Nevada (top); hot spring,*
Yellowstone National Park (bottom)

TABLE OF CONTENTS

WAITING FOR THE WATER

You hear a hiss of **steam**. Boiling water roars. A jet of water shoots into the air. Old Faithful is **erupting**! It is one of the most reliable geysers in the world!

OLD FAITHFUL, YELLOWSTONE NATIONAL PARK

BOILING OVER

A geyser forms when hot rocks deep in the earth make water boil. The water collects in a **reservoir**. When it boils, it needs to escape.

The water follows cracks in the earth to a small opening on the surface. Then it shoots up into the air.

RED-HOT MAGMA

Conditions must be just right for a geyser to form. That is why they are **rare**. There are only about 1,000 geysers.

The heat from **magma** makes geysers possible. There have to be cracks in the ground, too.

cone geyser

CASTLE GEYSER

fountain geyser

STROKKUR

GEYSER GUIDE

There are two types of geysers. Fountain geysers look like pools of water. They erupt like an explosion. Cone geysers are gentler. They spray water in steady jets.

HOT SPOTS

About half of the world's geysers are in Yellowstone National Park in Wyoming. There are between 300 and 500 active geysers there. Russia, Chile, and Iceland also have many geysers.

VALLEY OF GEYSERS, RUSSIA

FAMOUS GEYSERS

The Strokkur geyser in Iceland erupts every 6 to 10 minutes. It can shoot water 100 feet (30.5 m) into the air.

YELLOWSTONE'S CASTLE GEYSER

Yellowstone's Old Faithful erupts about 20 times a day. If you take a hike in Yellowstone, you will probably see a geyser. They are worth the wait!

ACTIVITY: MAKE A GEYSER

Materials

Water

Aluminum foil

Medium saucepan

Plastic funnel

1. Fill the pot with water.

2. Place the funnel upside down in the water, so the wide end is at the bottom.

3. Cover the pot with aluminum foil, cutting a hole for the spout of the funnel.

4. Ask an adult to help you turn on the heat under the pot and bring the water to a boil.

5. Stand a safe distance away from the pan and watch the steam come out of the funnel spout—and then the water, too!

GLOSSARY

erupting: for geysers, becoming active and letting off hot water and steam

magma: hot liquid rock beneath the earth's surface

rare: not found in large numbers

reservoir: a place where a liquid collects

steam: the vapor that is formed when water is heated

READ MORE

Bryan, T. Scott. *Geysers: What They Are and How They Work*. 2nd ed. Missoula, Mont.: Mountain Press, 2005.

Llewellyn, Claire. *Geysers*. Chicago: Heinemann Library, 2000.

WEBSITES

Easy Science for Kids: Geysers and Hot Springs

http://easyscienceforkids.com/all-about-geysers-and-hot-springs/

Read more about geysers and see pictures of Old Faithful.

Science for Kids: Geysers for Kids

http://www.scienceforkidsclub.com/geysers.html

Learn more about how geysers are formed.

Note: Every effort has been made to ensure that any websites listed above were active at the time of publication and suitable for children. However, because of the nature of the Internet, it is impossible to guarantee that these sites will remain active indefinitely or that their contents will not be altered.

INDEX